I Am the Resurrection

Reginald Rice

Published by 7th Sign Publishing
peauxeticexpressions.com
Book Cover Design by David Boyce
Typesetting by Stewart A. Williams
Copyright ©2021 by Reginald Rice

ISBN – 13:978-0-578-99920-3
Printed in the United States
Rice, Reginald
I Am the Resurrection
All rights reserved. No part of this book may be reproduced or transmitted in any form or by any means without written permission from the author/and or publisher.

CONTENTS

Acknowledgements v

Dedication vi

Chapter 1 viii

Chapter 2 3

Chapter 3 6

Chapter 4 11

Chapter 5 15

Chapter 6 17

Chapter 7 19

Chapter 8 21

Chapter 9 24

Chapter 10 29

ACKNOWLEDGEMENTS

First, I thank my glorious and most gracious heavenly father and sweet Jesus Christ for receiving my confessions and the forgiveness of my sins!

The atonement of His holy blood, by the baptizing of the Father, the Son, and the Holy Spirit who bears recording heaven and the spirit and the water and the blood and these three agree in one (1 John 5:7-8), and the gates of heaven were opened for me, for citizenship, the gifts of Christ by the spirit of God descending like a dove and lighting upon me (Matthew 3:16).

Then I must thank 7th Sign Publishing, for believing that I'm blessed by God to relate His love towards His beautiful creations with a prophetic revelation. This book uses biblical scriptures and insight that wasn't given to today's priests. We all have been called as the Body of Christ to tend to His sheep and lambs. We have a certain gift and revelation that's for the edifying, exhortation and salvation of His people.

May this book bless you and touch you with the love of God, Christ and the Holy Spirit! I pray that the spirit opens the eyes in your heart and mind with understanding! I pray that you receive what God wants you to see and understand. Today is the day of salvation! For the kingdom of heaven is at hand!

DEDICATION

I dedicate this book to my sweet Jesus, my Lord, my Savior, my God! Thank you master for your holy blood and your holy spirit. Thank you for the light and eternal life....

For great is the mercy of the Lord of spirits. Long suffering is He and all His works, and all His power. Great are the things which He has done, has He revealed to the saints and to the elect in the name of the Lord of spirits. He will call to me, you are my father, my God, and the rock of my salvation! I openly receive God's promise and choose to stand here, humbly on God's promises and in worship of His person. Surely, the Lord God will do nothing, but he revealed His secret unto His servants, the prophets (Amos 3:7).

Chapter 1

Jesus said unto her, "I am the resurrection, and the life. He who believes in Me, though he were dead, yet shall he live and whosoever lives and believes in Me shall never die (John 11:25-26)."

Jesus Christ has given me insight and has revealed the mystery of the gospel and principalities, against powers, against the rulers of the darkness of this world and against spiritual wickedness in high places. Evil is a spiritual attack against the elect of God and Christ, profoundly to steal, kill, and destroy. The total objective is once you receive the holy spirit, Satan entices you with the greatest stronghold that you desire and enjoy as a sinner, hoping to turn you back into a slave of sin. Satan knows if the saint turns his back on God, serves him only and does not repent, the backslider will have no place with God and Christ. Hell will be their place for all eternity.

Hell is a real place. Never for once disbelieve that God wouldn't do such a thing to His people creation, God is Holy and created man in His image and that's to be holy (Numbers 16:1-22). – Korah committed rebellion and assembled against Moses and Aaron, and the earth opened its mouth and swallowed them up with their households and all the men with Koran with all their goods. So, they and all those with them went down alive into the pit, the earth closed over them and they perished from among the assembly. If you haven't received Jesus Christ as your lord and savior, you will pay for your rebellion against Christ the Lord!

The angels who kept not their first estate, but left their own habitation, He (the Lord) has reserved in everlasting chains under darkness unto the judgment of the great day Jude....

(Luke 16:22-24) And it came to pass, that the beggar died and was carried by the angels into Abraham's bosom. The rich man also died, and was buried and in hell he lift up his eyes being in torments, and sees Abraham afar off, and Lazarus in his bosom and he cried and said, father Abraham, have mercy on me, and send Lazarus that he may dip the tip of his finger, and cool my tongue, for I am tormented in this flame.

Christ has said that He will come like a thief in the night and you will not know the hour or day. Why? Because 99% of the time, the thief comes when you are asleep, and you know not what he taketh until you awake (Matthew 24:42-44), and if you die in your sleep without Christ, then when you awake will be before the great throne of God, and you must realize that if you're not written in the book of life, then death and hell were cast into the lake of fire.

This is the second death and whoever was not found written in the book of life was cast in the lake of fire. Why? Because you don't have the spirit of Christ! But if you continue to read this book, you will receive the Lord's gifts and become a beautiful jewel of Christ if you apply the instructions that I present to you, anointed by the author of the spirit for the Lord has said that he wishes for no one to perish, but that all should come to repentance (2 Peter 3:9).

He who loves his life shall lose it! Why? Because you love yourself more than the gift of God, which is Christ, meaning that you are of the world and fulfill the desires of the flesh, having not the spirit of God...Christ says. He who hates his life in this world shall keep it unto life eternally. Why? Because you realize that you're a sinner and you need the son of God to be made new. Amen (John 12:25).

Jesus...

I have come that they might have life, and that they may have it more abundantly (John 10:10)!

Come unto me, all you who labor and are heavily laden, and I will give you rest. Take my yoke upon you and learn of me; for I am meek and lowly in heart; and Ye shall find rest unto your souls. For my yoke is easy, and my burden is light (Matthew 11:28-30).

Chapter 2

Then God said, "Let there be light." And God saw the light, that it was good; and God divided the light from the darkness (Genesis 1:3-4).

When Adam was created, there was no darkness in him, and he lived in the presence of God, for God-Elohim was his light! Adam knew of no evil or sin, Adam was God's perfect creation, created and formed of the image of God-Elohim.

And the Lord God commanded the man (Adam) saying, "Of every tree of the garden you may freely eat, but of the tree of knowledge, of good and evil you shall not eat, for in the day that you eat of it you shall surely die (meaning spiritually die, which destroys the life of the flesh) (Genesis 2:16-17).

Adam was rebellious and disobeyed God. He and his wife Eve had taken and eaten the fruit of the tree of knowledge, of good and evil, so sin became of the first man and all men from him, which is a breaking of divine or moral law, which caused a divine separation from God and man, and man has no life without the presence of God-Elohim, and His presence is divine which is holy and spiritually consecrated (Genesis 3:1-24).

Now all men walked in darkness because of Adam, but there were God-fearing men who walked after Adam and sought the Lord God and His ways. Enoch is the first stated after Adam to have a one-on-one relationship with God, other than Abel who was killed by his brother Cain. (Genesis 5:24). Enoch walked with God, and he was not, for God took him. I would suggest that you read the book of Enoch, for it is a treasure to those who walk by faith, not by sight.

And the Lord, Adonbi said, "My spirit shall not strive with man forever, for he is indeed flesh, no-longer spiritual death (Genesis 6:3)." Man wasn't created to die! We were made and formed in the image of God, which God lives forever! We were created to live forever, and God-Elohim loves us so much that, He offers you and I his divine spirit again and the gift of life to live always and forever again by and through the man Jesus Christ. For God so loved the world that he gave His only begotten son, that whosoever believes in Him should not perish, but have everlasting life. (John 3:16), (Genesis 1:26-28).

To give knowledge of salvation unto his people by the remission of their sins. Through the tender mercy of our God, whereby the day springs from on high has listed us to give light to them who sit in darkness and in the shadow of death, to guide our feet into the way of peace (Luke 1:77-79), which would be done by Jesus going to the cross, another name for Christ," the day springs from on high, Jesus is the light of the world.

AND THE POWER OF DARKNESS

The light of the body is the eye; if therefore your eye be single, your whole body shall be full of light. But if your eye be evil, your whole body shall be full of darkness (Matthew 6:22-23).

What you take into your eyes is the mirror of your soul. What you take into your eyes effects your heart and emotions. So, lust will destroy you! Rather it's greed, money, fornication, or of the flesh, which is of the flesh and so it's not a holy thing. These things contribute to the spirit of darkness in you. Demonic strongholds keep you in sin, which cause you to walk condemned - at any time it could be for eternally.

A lost soul and a spirit of darkness shall dwell with those of its kind and at the appointed time you will acknowledge your rebellion, you will acknowledge and understand the torment of your being and you shall see him, Satan, for who he is and all those who served him because he is darkness and there is no light in him. He's like a magician who plays tricks on your eyes and your mind, anything to capture your interest to captivate your passion of all ungodliness to keep you from the kingdom of light but keep you in the kingdom of darkness! The deep bottom under the earth in the midst thereof, always and forever! For all eternally with pain and torment of hell fire for serving the enemy of God and denying the son of God, which is Christ.

Chapter 3

In Him was life, and the life was the light of men. And the light shines in darkness, and the darkness comprehended it not (John 1: 4-5).

Jesus! The spirit of life for all men. For unto us a son is given, and the government shall be upon his shoulder and his name shall be called wonderful counselor. The mighty God. The everlasting Father. The prince of peace (Isaiah 9:6). He alone is the life of source of light, if one doesn't know Christ one is in darkness. The light today shines all over the world and one day soon, there will be nothing left but that light and the sons of light.

That was the true light, which lighteth every man who comes into the world. He was in the world and the world was made by Him and the world knew Him not. He came unto his own, and his own received him not. But as many received Him, to them gave. He had the power to become the sons of God, even to them who believe on his name, Jesus Yahvahshua (John 1: 9-12).

Jesus is the only true light, if man is to find light, it will only be in Christ. The world cannot know Jesus by wisdom, but only by revelation. Faith in Jesus Christ and what he has done for us on the cross and believing in Him makes us sons of God. "Believe" is an action word. Act on the belief of Christ and follow His command.

He who believes in Him is not condemned but he who believes not is condemned already, because he has not believed in the name of the only begotten son of God and this is the condemnation that light is come into the world, and men loved darkness rather than light because their deeds were evil. For everyone who does evil hates the light. Either cometh to the light, lest His deeds should be reproved. But he does truth comes to the light, that his deeds may be made manifest, that they are wrought in God (John 3: 18-21).

Those who belong to Christ, blessed are you in all things and in every way! Yet we are not condemned to be eternally lost in the lake of fire forever (Revelations 20:11-15). All this refers to Christ and what He did at the cross in order to redeem humanity, salvation is never by works, but rather by grace through faith, with the cross ever the object of that faith, Jesus is the light and it's through Him that we become lights!

The fact that the great penalty of sin is sinful desire, the love of darkness is the consequence of man's wicked ways, the rejection of Jesus Christ is not the occasion of man's lostness, but rather the result of it. To truly come to Jesus means the revelation and condemnation of every evil way, which is totally unlike the religions of the world which reveal nothing, the "light" automatically reveals what is hidden by the darkness. The desire for truth must be placed in the heart of man by the holy spirit, by the means of the revealed word of God. If the person sincerely wants to do truth, he must come to Christ, for Christ is the only "light". The great change that takes place in the believing sinner's life upon coming to Christ, the evil deeds are forever gone.

Then Jesus said unto them, yet a little while is the light with you. Walk while you have the light, lest darkness come upon you, for he who walks in darkness knows where he goes. While you have the light, believe in the light, that you may be the children of light (John 12:35-36).

Jesus is the light and that light is the holy spirit! We receive the holy spirit through Christ, and we are lights in this world! We have eternal life, because of this light, indeed man must receive this light!

For you were sometimes in darkness, but now are you light in the Lord, walk as children of light (Eph 5:8). Everyone who doesn't know Christ is in spiritual darkness, and us that belong to Christ, we are a reflection of the light, spiritually and as a man. But all things that are reproved are made manifest by the light, for whosoever does make manifest is light. Wherefore, he said, awake though who sleeps, and arise from the dead, and Christ shall give you light (Ephesians 5:13-14).

It is only Christ and the cross which can adequately portray what sin. That's the reason many churches don't care for the cross. The cross alone manifests sin and all its evil affects. The light in you will reveal all sinful nature that tempts you or what you battle with spiritually. The holy spirit in you will give you discernment with people's spirits; this is a gift of the light.

Giving thanks unto the Father, who has made us meet to be partakers of the inheritance of the saints in light. Who has delivered us from the power of darkness and has translated us into the kingdom of his dear son (Colossians 1:12-13).

We must realize how important and special it is to have the light of Jesus Christ! This light makes us like Him in this world. Christ is still on earth in you and me! We are His spiritual body, He really lives in us, and there's no death, only this sinful flesh that we are in. But one day and that can be today, we shall be like Him and see Him for who He is.

But you brethren are not in darkness, that day should overtake you as a thief. You are the children of light and the children of day. We are not of night or of darkness (1 Thessalonians 5:4-5). But you are a chosen generation, a royal priesthood, a holy nation, a peculiar people, that you should show forth the praises of him who has called you out of darkness into His marvelous light (1 Peter 2:9).

We are a holy family, a family who has power, a family that belongs to the living God. Our greatest power is love and faith endures all things! Praise the Father of spirits, for He is great and deserves to be praised.

This is the message which we have of Him and declare unto you that God is light and in him is no darkness. But if we walk in the light, as He is in the light, we have fellowship one with another (1 John 1:5-7). God separates the light from the darkness, the waters above from the waters below, the sea form the dry land. He places lights in the firmament to distinguish day from night. Then God sets apart the sabbath from other days and calls it holy. God separates what is good.

Chapter 4

Today is the last day! Rather you have Christ or you belong to Satan, because if you die right now, that's who you belong to, and there's no mercy before God on the day of His judgment (Revelations 20:11-15).

Jesus said, but as touching the resurrection of the dead have you not read that which was spoken unto you by God, saying I am the God of Abraham, Isaac and the God of Jacob! God is not the God of the dead, but of the living (Matthew 22: 31-32). This scripture guarantees our resurrection as well as life after death.

There's no spiritual death in Christ! The spirit is what lives in a man, and if you have the holy spirit, which is the spirit of Christ, when your fleshly body dies, you will continue to live before Go. There's no death in Christ, only the spirit of Adam, which we no longer have when we receive the holy spirit.

This is the Father's will which has sent me, that all of which he has given me. I should lose nothing but should raise it up again at the last day (John 6:39).

Today is that last day! I guarantee you, if you belong to Jesus Christ, and you die today, you will be with Christ in His kingdom. It's impossible for the holy spirit to be on hold in the ground. The holy spirit that's in you shall return where it came from in heaven from the kingdom of God-Elohim.

And you shall know the truth, and the truth shall make you free (John 8:32). This is the secret of all abundant life in Christ. The truth is Jesus Christ and Him crucified. Which in Him alone is the way of salvation it makes you free from all things, you've been redeemed from mankind and you are now a God-kind.

Verily, verily, I say unto you if a man keeps my saying, he shall never see death (John 8:51).

PERSONAL REVELATION

In the year 2008, I did a four-day fast with no food, only water. On the 14th day, I awoke and my eyes opened. I saw within my soul and spirit that I was dying! So, I was fighting in my body to wake up but I couldn't wake up from the dying that was taking place. Suddenly, someone or something appeared before me. As I looked up and down, I was frightened and terrified thinking that something evil was about to happen to me. I kept looking and saw a robe with different colored jewels on it. I looked at his head, covered with the robe.

Then, he extended his hand towards me. I began to reach for his hand, smiling, and before I could touch him, he motioned with his hands. Then I woke up. I wondered for many days what the interpretation was for the vision.

The spirit revealed to me one day that when I die, The Lord, Christ will be right there to receive me and take me home.

The first resurrection is now! Indeed, if you have the holy spirit, the resurrection is in you. But now is Christ, risen from the dead and became the first-fruits of them who slept (1 Corinthians 15:20). For as in Adam all die, even so in Christ shall all be made alive. But every man in his own order in Christ. The first-fruits afterward they who are Christ's at His coming (1 Corinthians 15: 22-23).

WHO ARE FIRST FRUITS?

Those who are or have been baptized into the spirit, which is called Pentecost (Acts 2:1-13). These are our brothers and sisters who have been born again by the womb of God. So, when we die, we are before the Lord, which is considered the first fruits of his body (Revelations 14:1-5).

Yavahshua Ma Moshiach of Nazareth. Are the 144,000 the only ones that are saved and belong to Jesus? For your own curiosity, you need to read Revelations 5:9-10 and Revelations 7: 9-10.

We must realize we are called to be servants of the Lord, just like Moses was called out from among God's people to lead the whole nation of Israel from Pharaoh out of the bondage of slavery and Egypt. The same goes for Christ and His body. Servants are called from His body to lead His people into the promised land like Moses, but our promised land is the kingdom of God and His kingdom on earth and just like the Israelites inherit the land,

Christians shall inherit the earth (Matthew 5:5).

And God has set some in the church, first apostles, secondarily prophets, thirdly teachers, after that, miracles, then gifts of healings, helps, governments, diversities of tongue (1 Corinthians 12: 28).

And he gave some apostles and some prophets and some evangelists and some pastors and teachers (Ephesians 4:11). These are our brothers and sisters ordained by the holy spirit and taught by the holy spirit to conduct these offices, unlike one who attends seminary classes and receives ordainment, which is a love and dedication towards God. When the spirit calls and ordains, it's a greater call than man to man ordainment.

The five-fold ministry that is or called out from among the body of Christ, serves these offices until they die in the flesh and no more on earth. There's no retirement from serving God and His people. Every person in the Bible served God and Christ until they were killed or died! Some seminary graduates retire or uses the services of Christ as a profession or employment for financial gains.

Surely, there's condemnation for those who peddle the word of God. Some people play with the Lord's money and misuse His congregation's spiritual and financial needs. A true man of God approves himself to the Lord by keeping his commandments and servicing his people. So, thank God for the holy spirit because it restores us and makes first fruits according to the hearts of men who were predestined to this calling.

Chapter 5

And it shall come to pass that whoever shall call on the name of the Lord shall be saved (Acts 2:21).

Now is the day of salvation (2 Corinthians 6:2). Today is the day to approach the Son of God, with a confession of a sinner, and welcome Him into your life. Become saved from condemnation of eternal fire.

What must I do to be saved? And they said believe in the Lord, Jesus Christ, and you shall be saved, and your house (Acts 16:30-31).

That if you shall confess with your mouth the Lord Jesus and shall believe in your heart that God has raised Him from dead, you shall be saved. For with the heart man believes unto righteousness and with the mouth confession is made unto salvation (Romans 10: 9-10).

You will not be ashamed of faith and hope. Trust in the Lord with all your heart, your might, and soul and you shall be blessed in all things, because He promises us these things (Deuteronomy 28 and 30).

All who the Father gives me shall come to me and him who comes to me I will in no wise case out (John 6:17). Repent and be baptized, every one of you in the name of

Jesus Christ for the forgiveness of your sins and you will receive the gift of the holy spirit (Acts 2:38).

RECEIVE SALVATION – CONFESS ALOUD NOW

Jesus Christ, I ask you to forgive me Lord of all the evil, wicked sins I've ever committed in my life. I ask you to come in my heart. Purge me, cleanse me, and make me new! I ask you to live in my heart!

I accept you as my Lord and Savior! I believe and know that you are the son of God! I believe and know that God did raise you from the dead. I am saved.

    I say unto you that likewise joy shall be in heaven over the sinner who repents (Luke 15:7). An angel in heaven blows his trumpet announces salvation on earth. The whole heavenly kingdom of God knows about you. Praise the Lord. You are saved.

Chapter 6

And behold, I send the promise of my father upon you (Luke 24:49).

The baptism with the holy spirit which was first given on the day of Pentecost (Acts 1:4-5).

If you love me, keep my commandments. And I will pray to the Father and He shall give you another comforter, that He may abide with you forever. Even the spirit of truth, whom the world cannot receive because it seems Him not, neither knows Him but you know Him for He dwells with you and shall be in you. (John 14:15-17). The spirit gives life (2 Corinthians 3:6).

You'll never die! What lives is what lives inside you. This flesh is sinful but the new body we put on is holy. Hereby, we know that we dwell in Him, and He in us because, He has given us of His spirit (1 John 4:13). If so be that the spirit of God dwell in you. Now if any man has not the spirit of Christ, he is none of His. And if Christ be in you the body is dead because of sin but the spirit is life because of righteousness (Romans 8: 9-10; also read Romans 8:1-9; 8:11-17).

ASK GOD FOR THE HOLY SPIRIT

How much more shall your heavenly father give the holy spirit to them who ask Him (Luke 11:13)?

Heavenly Father, in the name of Jesus, I ask for the holy spirit. Create in me a clean heart O'God and renew a right spirit within me (Psalms 51:10).

Christ, not by water only, but by water and blood. And it is the spirit who bear witness, because the spirit is truth (1 John 5:6).

Eternal Father, wonderful counselor. I ask that you touch this person's heart and give understanding to their heart and mind, for the glory of your son Jesus. Now this I say, brethren, that flesh, and blood cannot inherit the kingdom of God (1 Corinthians 15:50).

We must receive His spirit, God Yahvah, He who exists, the adorable one.

Chapter 8

FOLLOW ME (MATTHEW 9:9).

Whosoever shall confess me before men, him will I confess also before my Father which is in heaven. But whosoever shall deny me before men, him I will also deny before my Father which is in heaven (Matthew 10:32-33).

In this world today that we live in, it's critical every person walks in their own way and by what seems right in their own eyes but their end is eternal destruction. Jesus is not a factor to a lot of people. They do not fear the Lord enough to love Him and keep His ways! The world is caught up in self-pleasure and is spiritually blind, and we know when the blind follows the blind, they fall into the ditch (Matthew 15:14), and that ditch is hell.

There are more people that serve the world than God, from every sport that is being played daily, there is a full attendance of hundreds of thousands of people, praising athletes and sports, with all their heart, might, and soul. Sporting events receive more attendance than church! America is lost in the sauce, no longer fearing God. No longer valuing God's laws and principles, as long as

America is happy.

The inhabitants of one city shall go to another, saying let us go speedily to pray before the Lord, and to seek the Lord of hosts. I will go also. Yea, many people and strong nations shall come to seek the Lord of hosts in Jerusalem, and to pray before the Lord. Thus saith the Lord of hosts in those days it shall come to pass that ten men shall take hold out of all languages of the nations, even shall take hold of the skirt of Him that is a Jew, saying we will go with you, for we have heard that God is with you (Zachariah 8:21-23).

People are lost and serving God how they want to serve Him, instead of His statutes. I'm full gospel, but I do agree with serving God and the Christ with the love of Enoch, Ndah, Abraham, Isaac and Jacob, Moses, Elijah, Elisha and King David. Pure love. Pure dedication. Solid faith.

Jesus said, if any man will come after me, let him deny himself, and take up his cross, and follow me. For whosoever shall save his life shall lose it, and whosoever will lose his life for my sake shall find it (Matthew 16:24-25)

IS CHRIST DIVIDED (1 CORIANTHIANS 1:13)?

There is no separation in Christ. All these different denominations can take away from the main goal, serving Christ according to the gospel. Denominations are a demonic attack from Satan and the men of God, quote, unquote allowed the enemy to use them in a way where they could be seen. The reason why different denominations are demonically influenced is because each denomination disagrees with one another; there's hatred among the brethren and divisions.

The word of God says this:

He who says he is in the light and hates his brother is in darkness even until now. But he who hates his brother is in darkness and walks in darkness (1 John 2:9,11).

He who loves not his brother abides in death. Whosoever hates his brother is a murderer and you know that no murderer has eternal life abiding in him (1 John 3:14-15).

Stan first objective after being defeated by the cross is the church. All different ways of believing and serving Christ idolatry with the beads and hail Marys, Christ is not God denying the Christ! The Anti-Christ Satan ministers marry same sex couples in the house of God, making a mockery of God. God will not be mocked (Galatians 6:7). Surely you bring condemnation upon yourself, playing with the Lord, leaning upon thine own understanding (Proverbs 3:5).

Let us with spiritual understanding pray for our brothers and sisters who have gone astray from the Lord by being misled by false prophets and preachers. Let us pray that God saves His people, the lambs of Christ, who has been taught in error and these teachers with no spiritual insight from the ghost, accursed they are and shall be.

Christ is the center of salvation. Him alone and once we've received His forgiveness, we became sons of God even Him, the Father of Christ-Elohim Elshaddai! God Almighty.

Chapter 9

THE BACKSLIDER IN HEART SHALL BE FILLED WITH HIS OWN WAYS (PROVERBS 14:14).

Thine own wickedness shall correct thee, and thy backslidings shall reprove thee; know therefore and see that it is an evil thing and bitter, that thou hast forsaken the Lord thy God, and that my fear is not in thee, Saith the Lord God of hosts (Jeremiah 2:19).

My dear brother or sister, if you have strayed away from the Lord, now is the time to amend your differences with the Lord, He's once said: I will heal their backsliding. I will love them freely, for mine anger is turned away from (Hosea 19:4).

He looks for our return! He embraces our return. The word says in Isaiah 55:7, Let the wicked forsake his way, and the unrighteous man his thoughts and let him return into the Lord-Adonai, and He will have mercy upon him: and to our God, for He will do abundantly, pardon.

Return, ye backsliding children, and I will heal your backslidings, behold, we come unto thee, for thou art the Lord-Adonai our God (Jeremiah 3:22).

The Lord holds no grudges with you. We serve a merciful God. They say that He is full of compassion and rich in mercy (Lamentations 3:21-23).

For it is impossible for those who were once enlightened and have tasted of the heavenly gift and were made partakers of the spirit and have tasted the good word of God, and the powers of the world to come. If they shall fall away, to renew them again unto repentance, seeing they crucify to themselves the son of God afresh, and put Him to an open shame (Hebrews 6:4-6).

We must come back to repentance. Purge our hearts! Purify our hearts from all evilness, wickedness of sin, and allow the holy spirit to cleanse us so that we are able to walk in the spirit (Galatians 5:22-23).

If we confess our sins, He's faithful and just to forgive us of our sins and to cleanse us from all unrighteousness (1 John 1:9).

THE BACKSLIDER'S PRAYER

Heavenly Father in the name of Jesus Christ!

I have sinned. I have fallen back into a rebellious state of being. I realize and understand my faults Father God. I am so remorseful and convicted for breaking our covenant and fellowship.

Create in me a clean heart, o' God, and renew a right spirit within me. Cast me not away from thy presence and take not thy holy spirit from me. Purge me with hyssop, and I shall be clean. Wash me, and I shall be whiter than snow.

Heavenly Father "Yah", forgive me for all the sins I have committed during my rebellion. Jesus Christ, forgive me for defiling your blood, your body and our communion. Lord, I ask you to cleanse my heart with your blood. Lord cleanse my mind with your blood. Living blood of Jesus Christ, I welcome you to cleanse my thoughts. Cleanse the intentions of my thinking. Cleanse my eyes Holy Blood of Jesus Christ and my hidden sins. Forgive me for defiling your holy spirit, your body, and your temple. Holy Spirit, forgive me for grieving you and disrespecting you with association of Satan and darkness. Father, you promised to forgive me. So, I am forgiven! Jesus, you said that all whom come unto you, by no means will cast him out! Holy Spirit, I hear your voice, therefore I will not harden my heart, and I welcome your inner presence of residence. In Jesus' name, Amen.

DELIVERANCE MINISTRY

I repent, for the kingdom of heaven is at hand. Jesus said in his name, heal the sick, cleanse the lepers, raise the dead, cast out devils, freely ye receive, freely give. Indeed, if I cast out devils by the spirit of God, then the kingdom of God has come upon you. Jesus, the son of God, has given His disciples power and authority over all unclean spirits, to cast them out and to heal all manner of sickness and diseases. Christ defeated Satan on the cross much more than being now justified by His blood! Let every soul be subject unto the higher powers, for there is no power but of God!

But he who is spiritual judges all things, yet he himself is judged of no man. For who has known the mind of the Lord, that he may instruct him, but we have the mind of Christ, in whom we have redemption through His blood, the forgiveness of sins, and having made peace through the blood of His cross, by Him to reconcile all things unto himself.

The weapons of our warfare are not carnal, but mightily in God for pulling down strong holds, casting down arguments and every high thing that exalts itself against the knowledge of God. I will remind you of Satan's failure and Jesus' victory. The God of peace crushes you, Satan, under my feet!

God has not given me a spirit of fear, but of power and of love and of a sound mind. In the name of Jesus, I expel you spirit of fear! I expel you spirit of lies! I expel you spirit of darkness in the name of Jesus! Perverted spirit, I expel you in the name of Jesus and command you to come out! Spirit of witchcraft, I expel you and command you to come out in the name of Jesus of Nazareth!

I have been crucified with Christ. It is no longer I who lives, but Christ who lives in me. For I have died and my life is hidden with Christ in God.

Spirit of deception, I expel you in the name of Jesus! Spirit of delusions, I expel you in the name of Jesus! Spiritual conflict of this kind is not the evidence of failure, rather it is an essential condition for fruitful ministry, because demonic spirits are active and real against the children of God and their election to the kingdom of God.

Apostle Paul says that in Ephesians 6:12, for we wrestle,

not against the flesh and blood but against principalities, against powers, the rulers of darkness in this world, against spiritual wickedness in high places. But we are more than conquerors in Christ (Romans 8:37).

Chapter 10

PERSONAL ANOINTED PRAYERS CONSECRATED AND WRITTEN ON A 10 DAY FAST

Elohim-God-Yahvah, the eternal one who saves Yahvahshua – Jesus, Son of Elohim who redeems.

Your son came before you, before thy throne of grace, exalting you, worshipping your persons, giving you praise and honor, you are the Lord thy God and I petition you, also inquire of the Lord. As I proclaim my fast as the body of Christ. I pray for the anointing of the spirit and I seek a word of wisdom-for accomplishing your will in given situations as well as my future, Father I ask for a word of knowledge, revelation of the divine will and plan in my life, Elohim most high.

I pray for supernatural faith; the ability to believe you in all things without doubt. I proclaim a miracle of faith, supernatural faith, working of miracles to overcome evil obstacles, Satan and sickness. I pray for the gift of supernatural healing, God's gift to men, for the glory of Christ, I pray for the power of the spirit, to preach and teach the gospel of Jesus Christ – to evangelize with authority, missionaries of the Lord – Adonai. I pray for restoration

Holy Father, to commit myself to the discipleship works of Christ! Allow me to walk and live according to my created purpose. Make my Lord and Savior, Jesus Christ proud of me, and that His holy blood truly has power towards the sinner. In Jesus' name, I pray and ask these things of you Father. Amen.

PRAYER TWO

Lord of Spirits – My Divine Master –
All Sufficient El Shaddai

This shall we do in the fear of the Lord, faithfully and with a perfect heart. I serve you and love you!

Holy Father, I pray to be righteous in your sight. Father, I pray and seek you in the days of Jesus, and I pray for understanding in the visions of God. As long as I seek the Lord God, make me to prosper and in every work that I began in the service of the House of God and in the commandments to seek my God, I shall do it with all my heart and prosper.

Surely, the Lord God will do nothing but he revealeth his secrets unto his servants the prophets. So, I pray for spirit discernment. Everything I need to glorify your son and to the edification, exhortation and salvation unto men. Help me oh Lord! Assist me, as I seek and walk in your holy will in all things with Christ and my personal life as a son of God. The word says if we draw near to you, that you will draw near to us!

Jesus said, all that come unto him by no means would he cast them away. Use me Lord, let the anointing of the spirit and favor from you, that I may attract men who need you! Let the gospel of Jesus Christ be in my heart, my mind, on my tongue, in my walk and with power of the spirit, with demonstration. In Jesus' name I pray and ask these things Lord Master, amen.

PRAYER THREE

The Lord that health thee! I'm at your mercy, wonderful Father and Sweet Lord Christ

You wound and you heal. Have mercy on me, o' Lord for I am weak, o' Lord. Heal me, for my bones are troubled. Who forgiveth all thine iniquities, who healeth all thy diseases. He sent His word and healed them and delivered them from destruction. But he was wounded for our transgressions. He was bruised for our iniquities, the chastisement of our peace was upon Him, and with His stripes we are healed (according to your word by Isaiah the prophet).

Then shall thy light break forth as the morning and thine health shall spring forth speedily and thy righteousness shall go before thee, thy glory of the Lord shall be by reward. Return ye back sliding children and I will heal your back slidings.

Behold, I come unto thee for thou art my God. Come and let us return unto the Lord, for He hath torn and He will heal us. He has smitten and He will bind us up. He will revive us after two days. In the third day He will raise us up and we shall live in His sight. But unto you that fear my name shall the sun of righteousness arise with the healing in His wings and ye shall go forth and grow up as calves of the stall.

And ye shall tread down the wicked, for they shall be

ashes under the soles of your feet. In the day that I shall do this, saith the Lord of hosts. Lord I believe but help my unbelief. Beloved, I wish above all things that thou mayest prosper and be in health even as thy soul prospereth. In Jesus' name, I receive this blessing. Amen.

PRAYER FOUR

El-shaddai. Holy One of Israel

Then the spirit of the Lord will come upon you and you will prophesy with them and be turned into another man in the name of Jesus! God, give me another heart and let all these signs come to pass for your glory! This day, make me a man of God. Lord you have pierced my heart. You have broken me! I am no longer rebellious towards you. Make me to be what you want me to be for you and your beloved son Jesus. For God made my heart weak, and the almighty terrifies me. The poor shall eat and be satisfied.

Those who seek Him will praise the Lord. Let your heart live forever. The king's heart is in the hand of the Lord, like the rivers of water. He turns it wherever he wishes. The heart is deceitful above all things, and desperately wicked. Who can know it? I, the Lord, search the heart. I test the mind, even to give every man according to his ways; according to the fruit of his doings. Then I will give them a heart to know me, that I am the Lord.

And they shall be my people, and I will be their God, for they shall return to me with their whole heart. Then I will give them one heart, and I will put a new spirit within them and take the stony heart out of their flesh and give them a heart of flesh. Cast away from you all the transgressions which you have committed and get yourselves a new heart and a new spirit.

Create in me a clean heart, o'God, and renew a steadfast spirit within me. Jesus, you said He who believes in you, as the scripture has said, out of his heart will flow rivers of living water. Dear Lord, cleanse my heart, heal my heart, bless my heart o'Lord. Purge my heart with your blood. Amen.

PRAYER FIVE

Adorable One – The Supreme Object of Worship God
In thee Lord, do I put my trust. Let me never be ashamed. Deliver me in thy righteousness. Bow down thine ear to me, deliver me speedily. Be thou my string rock for a house of defense to save me and hide not they face from thy servant. For I am in trouble. Hear me speedily. Draw nigh unto my soul and redeem it. Deliver me of mine enemies. Turn me again, o'God and cause thy face to shine and I shall be saved. Turn me unto thee, o'Lord. Turn though unto me and I shall be turned.

Renew my days as of old. Then they cried unto the Lord in their trouble and He delivered them out of their distresses. Call upon me in the day of trouble. I will deliver thee and thou shalt glorify me. I will go and return to my place til they acknowledge their offense and seek my face in their affliction. They will seek me early and shall not God avenge His own elect, which cry day and night unto Him, though he bear long with them? I tell you that He will avenge them speedily, says Jesus the Christ! Therefore, I say unto you, what things so ever ye desire, when ye pray, believe that ye receive them and ye shall have them. In Jesus' name, I shall receive these things, Amen.

PRAYER SIX

Holy Father, in the name of Jesus, I ask you: Now unto Him who is able to do exceedingly and abundantly above all that I ask or think according to the power that works in me. For the same Lord over all is rich unto all who call upon him. For I know the grace of our Lord, Jesus Christ that, though He was rich, yet for my sake he became poor, that I through His poverty might be rich. Both riches and honor come from you, o'Lord and you reign over all.

Worthy is the lamb that was slain to receive power and riches and wisdom and strength and honour and glory and blessings. Let the word of Christ dwell in you richly in all wisdom. Charge them who are in this world that they be not high minded nor trust in uncertain riches, but in the living God who gives us richly all things to enjoy that they do good, that they be rich in good works. Heavenly Father, bless me with the blessings that I've obtained, through your beloved son, Jesus Christ. Amen.

PRAYER SEVEN

Elahah – Elohim-El-Shaddai

Who is like you? Surely, you are one of a kind! Glorious, one majesty, honour, praise and worship belongs to you. I shall not come empty handed before the Lord. I only find that you find my labors towards the kingdom and discipleship work towards Christ, sufficient in its season and bless me according to any labor and my love dedication towards you and your son.

You said Holy Father, you will bless thee in all thy increase and in all the works of thine hands. Therefore, thou shalt surely rejoice. Be glad then, ye children of Zion, and rejoice in the Lord your God. For He hath given you the former rain moderately, and He will cause to come down for you, the rain, the former rain and the latter rain in the first month. And ye shall eat in plenty and be satisfies and praise the name of the Lord, your God, that hath dealt wondrously with you, and my people shall never be ashamed. So shall my word be that go forth out of my mouth, it shall not return unto me void, but it shall accomplish that which I please and it shall prosper in things whereto I sent it. Heaven and earth shall away but my words shall not pass away. But without faith it is impossible to please him. For he that cometh to God must believe that He is and that He is a rewarder of them that diligently seek Him. In Jesus' name, Amen.

PRAYER EIGHT
Elohim Thy Glorious One of Israel

I will trust in the Lord and do good, so shall thou dwell in the land and verily thou shall be fed. In thee, o' Lord, do I put my trust. Let me never be put to confusion, for thou art my hope! O' Lord God, thou art my trust from my youth, many sorrows shall be to the wicked, but he that trusts in the Lord, mercy shall compass him about. He trusted on the Lord, that He would deliver him, let Him deliver him, seeing He delighted in Him. Trust in the Lord with all thine heart, and lean not unto thine own understanding. He that trusteth in his own heart is a fool, but whoso walketh wisely, he shall be delivered.

Behold, God is my salvation, I will trust and not be afraid, for the Lord Jehovah is my strength and my song. He also has become my salvation. He trusted in God, let him deliver him now if he will have him. For he said, I am the son of God. That we should be to the praise of His glory, who first trusted in Christ. Let not mercy and truth forsake thee bind them about thy neck, write them upon the table of thine heart. Be not wise in thine own eyes, fear the Lord and depart from evil. The fear of the Lord is to hate evil, pride, and arrogancy and the evil way and the froward mouth, do I hate.

Blessed is the man that heareth me, watching daily at my gates, waiting at the posts of my doors. For whoso findeth me findeth life and shall obtain favor of the Lord. Thank you, Lord, for I trust in you and all your ways for surely there's no one like you. In Jesus, I trust and pray in His name, Amen.

PRAYER NINE

Heavenly Father, He Who Exists

I know that you are a restorer! I know that you will make my life much better than the former. I shall pray to God, and He will delight in Him. He shall see His face with joy, for He restores to man his righteousness. He restores my soul. He leads me in the path of righteousness, for His name's sake. Restore to me the joy of your salvation and uphold me by the generous spirit. Those who hate me without a cause are more than the hairs on my head.

They are mighty who would destroy me, being my enemies wrongfully. Though I have stolen nothing. I still restore it. For I will restore health to you and heal you of your wounds says the Lord. Because they called you an outcast and maybe to you a restorer of life, a nourisher of your old age.

Return to the stronghold, you prisoners of hope. Even today, I declare that I will restore double to you. In Jesus' name, let thy words come to pass. Then the Lord answered me and said write the vision and make it plain on tablets, that he may run who reads it. For the vision is yet for an appointed time. But at the end it will speak and it will not lie, though it tarries. Wait for it, because it will surely come; it will not tarry. With men this is impossible, but with God all things are possible, thus says the Lord.

PRAYER TEN

The Lord Bless Me

May Yahovah-Elohim, my heavenly Father (He who exists) kneel before me making himself available to me (like a good father kneeling before his child) in order to minister and bestow His gifts and promises. And keep me. May Yahovah-Elohim, my heavenly Father guard me with a hedge of thorny protection that will prevent Satan, and all my enemies from harming my body, my soul, my mind, and my spirit, my loved ones and all my possessions.

The Lord makes His face shine upon me. May Yahvan-Yahovan, my heavenly father illuminates the wholeness of His being toward me continually bringing me to order so that I will my God given destiny and purpose and be gracious to me. May Yahvah-Yahovah, my heavenly Father, lift up and carry His fullness of being toward me, bringing everything that He is to my aid, supporting me with His divine embrace and entire being and give me peace.

Set in place all I need to be whole and complete so I can walk in victory, moment by moment by the power of the spirit, may give me supernatural health, peace, welfare, safety, soundness, tranquility, prosperity, perfection, supernatural fullness, rest, harmony, as well as the absence of agitation and discord. In Jesus' name, thus saith the Lord, Amen.

Today is the resurrection in Jesus Christ.

And the graves were opened, and many bodies of the saints who had fallen asleep were raised, and coming out of the graves after His resurrection, they went into the holy city and appeared to many (Matthew 27:52).

> We are alive in Christ! The spirit is life!
> The kingdom is yours!
> May our Heavenly Father, Jesus Christ,
> and the holy spirit bless you.

Love always. Your brother in Christ
Reginald D. Rice
Priestly Office

www.ingramcontent.com/pod-product-compliance
Lightning Source LLC
Chambersburg PA
CBHW071846290426
44109CB00017B/1937

Chapter 7

And Jesus, when He was baptized, went up straight way out of the water, and lo, the heavens were opened unto Him, and He saw the spirit of God descending like a dove, and lighting upon Him (Matthew 3:16).

When we accept Jesus Christ as our Lord and Savior, and are baptized, the gates of heaven are open unto us, as the spirit descends upon us.

Jesus answered, "Verily, verily, I say unto you, except a man be born of water and of the spirit, he cannot enter into the kingdom of God. That which is born of the flesh is flesh, and that which is born of the spirit is spirit. Marvel not that I said unto you, you must be born again (John 3:5-7).

For there are three who bear record in heaven, the Father, the word, and the holy spirit, and these three are one. And there are three who bear witness in earth, the spirit, and the water and the blood: and these three agree in one (1 John 5:7-8).

When we are baptized, this above is an ordained spiritual agreement by God, because:

This is He who came by water and blood, even Jesus